JOURNEY BEYOND THE SELF

Vignettes of a seeker's life

Dr E.M. Martin

IngramSpark

Melbourne, VIC

Copyright © 2018 by **Dr E.M. Martin**

All rights reserved. Apart from fair dealing for the purposes of study, research, criticism or review as permitted under the Copyright Act, no part of this publication may be reproduced, distributed or transmitted in any form or by any means without prior written permission.

E.M. Martin/IngramSpark
www.emmartin.live
https://www.facebook.com/JourneyBeyondTheSelf

Publisher's note: This is a work of literary nonfiction. Every effort has been made to provide accurate source attribution. Should any attribution be found to be incorrect, the author/publisher welcomes written documentation supporting correction for subsequent printing. For material not in the public domain, selection was made according to generally accepted fair-use standards and practices.

Journey Beyond the Self: Vignettes of a Seeker's Life. -- 1st ed.
ISBN 978-0-6483856-0-8

Text editing and book design by Dr Juliette Lachemeier@The Erudite Pen: www.theeruditepen.com

Cover designed by Chris Hildenbrand

Dedicated to my master and teacher – my mother.

*'Wisdom is knowing I am nothing,
Love is knowing I am everything,
And between the two my life moves'*

——SRI NISARGADATTA MAHARAJ

CONTENTS

Part 1: Setting the Scene 1

1. Introduction.. 3

2. Journey into Oblivion 2015–2016 7

3. My Dreams: What is Real? 25

Part 2: Seeking in Earnest 37

4. Dark Night of the Soul: Journal Sept 2017–Mar 2018 39

Part 3: Nirvana 65

5. The Turning Point 67

6. An Illumined Exploration of Words 87

7. Epilogue 107

Part 1: Setting the Scene

1. Introduction

There is no story here, just a compilation of words, inspirations, events, dreams and snippets of a seeker's journey. A seeker of what, you may ask? Some call it enlightenment, some self-realisation and others refer to it as nirvana or an expansion of self into no self.

What I can tell you is that throughout this journey, I knew that I was seeking something, but did not know exactly what. All the existential questions plagued my being – Who am I? Why am I here? What is it all for? What is the purpose of this life? These vignettes will take you on this journey with me, traversing the darkness of the psyche and bringing it to the light of consciousness and beyond.

So we begin, and I will set the scene for you. Despite living an 'ideal' life by society's standards – with supportive loved ones, material comfort, good friends, a well-paid job and every measure of success – as far back as I can recall, a dissatisfaction of varying intensity and a feeling of emptiness has always been present deep within.

In this respect, 'I' have always been a seeker. The searching has always been there. Most of my life was spent looking for something, anything, because life was never quite 'right'. So the searching was here, there and everywhere for adventure, change, love, friendship, a career, self-destruction – anything that could ease the sense of unease and incompleteness within my being. But all the outward searching was to no avail. The feeling of dissatisfaction and emptiness always remained.

This sense of dissatisfaction and emptiness intensified a few years ago, and most of 2015 and 2016 were marked by acute anxiety. From 2015 onward, the feeling of emptiness intensified exponentially, enveloping every aspect of my life in an overwhelming feeling of separateness from the world around me. Other words to describe the experience are angst, depression, anxiety, suffering and pain. Every day on waking, the questions screamed in my consciousness: Who am I? Why am I here? What is it all for? What is the purpose of this life?

After three years of intensely seeking for answers, on March 19, 2018, something changed within me. What changed? That is what this book is about, and for you, the reader, to decide.

The pages in this book include vignettes of my experiences from 2015–2018. The book itself is divided into three parts. Part 1 sets the scene for my gradual dissolution of self during 2015–2016, which I have related through nine different poems and very vivid dream journals. Part 2 reveals my seeking in earnest and my darkest nights of the soul, as recorded in my journals from 2017–2018. Part 3 takes you on a journey with me through to a culmination point, which I have named nirvana. Nirvana is explored through journal entries, an illumined exploration of words and the insights into life, love and the nature of being that have been gleaned since my turning-point moment on March 19, 2018.

The vignettes speak of my journey essentially as one of the mind. The pages document a rollercoaster of suffering, depression and questioning, interspersed with moments of clarity and understanding until a 'space' started enveloping my consciousness.

As you read on, you will note that these moments of clarity become longer and longer, interspersed with days when the suffering mind kicked back in with its never-ending tirade of negativity. Slowly, the mind becomes quieter and quieter, until March 19th, 2018, when 'my' mind just gives up.

From this day onwards, the feelings of separateness, pain and suffering ended. Personally, it can be called *nirvana*, solely because the experience of being without suffering is *bliss* in itself.

What happened? Words inadequately describe the experience. Essentially, the journey was a disintegration of everything that defined me – a movement from self into no self. A journey into the vast spaciousness and consciousness that is beyond the 'myopic' self or ego. You can decide for yourself as you read.

Suffice to say, this could happen to any mind. My story could be your story.

E.M. Martin

2. Journey into Oblivion
2015–2016

Poems 1 – 9: Dissolution of Self

Poem 1

Corpse

How does God feel now?

Corpse, festering, burnt, decaying
pulling what's left of itself through
the scorching desert sand.

Driven by fear,
Fear of not succeeding,
unfulfilled expectations, goals, dreams, purpose.
Is this the carcass of my ancestral karma that I must
perpetuate?

Broken fingernails, rotting fingers propel
the carcass.

Searing pain, knowing the movement is desperate ...
useless. But trying anyway.

Ultimate suffering. Grasping for the mirage.
Productivity, efficiency, meaning, self.

My life has a PURPOSE,
doesn't it?

Who am I, if not that?

Every movement driven by MIND.
Where is God now?

Bipolar swings.
It will be okay. God is the doer.

Nothing is under control.
How can the mind ease itself?
It can't.

It fights, and fights, and fights
and screams, and cries, and
DOES NOT WANT TO DEAL WITH ITSELF ANY-
MORE.

Life is torture then.

Stinking, burning rotting corpse
suffering, agony, HELL fire.

Poem 2

Dust

Initiation.
Molten furnace.
Burning pain.
Despair.

A glimmer of relief
as the corpse looks up
and sees the vultures circling,
knowing that the end is nigh.

Can this body dissolve any faster?
I can't stand it anymore.

The corpse knowing it needs to let go.
The momentum has driven it
as far as it can go.

Stops, smiles to itself,
props itself up and looks into the SUN.

Vampiric end ...
Every atom of existence transmutes into dust.
Desert wind scatters the remains.

Consciousness fades into cool darkness.

Where am I now?

Nowhere ... everywhere.

What now?

Journey Beyond the Self   II

Poem 3

What now?

Open your eyes
What do you see?
Nothing has changed.
Everything has changed.

360 degrees and all dimensions.
An abyss of sorts.
Which way?
No need to ask.

Step into the abyss.
A rose will grow with every step.

Memories of the corpse, the pain and torture.
Flashbacks of that path.
The door has closed behind you.

What now?
Nothing but NOW.
Nothing exists but THIS.

Poem 4

A Taste

When the salt doll dissolves into the OCEAN,
When the bones disintegrate into the SAND,
What is the ocean and sand?

THIS is inevitability.
THIS is perfection.
THIS is DIVINITY.

MIND is gone
No mind to dictate, judge, control.
What is in place of MIND?

Inevitability,
Perfection,
Consciousness,
GOD.

Step into the abyss without looking down,
without wondering what is below, above, ahead.
Just step ...
There is ALWAYS a path.
The path of perfection.
The inevitable path.
Every speck of dust lands perfectly.
The sand and wind smile God's smile.

No more mind.
No more fighting.

This always was, but the mind was alive

and could not see
because it was always fighting.
It believed it was in control.
The definition of torture.

But we do not have to speak of that anymore.

Poem 5

Steps

Back to the suffering, NEVER!
There is nowhere else to go.
Hanging on the ledge ...
What if? What if? What if?

What if what?
What can be worse than the suffering, tortured
MIND?

Nowhere else to go.
Die if that is what follows, but
Never go back,
Impossible to go back.

Resignation to inevitability.
Nowhere else to go.
All avenues closed.
Exhaustion.

Eyes closed,
Fall forward into the ABYSS
Wanting to die.

A foot falls.
A path appears.
A rose grows.

Eyes open.
Sensory orientation.
Where is mind?

Quiet, watching, resting, peaceful
in the knowledge that it will
NEVER go back.

Smiling.
Another foot fall,
Another foot fall,
Roses bloom everywhere.

Relief
bursting.

Open the door
With eyes closed.
Step across the threshold
Eyes open.
The doorway disappears
behind.

Nothing exists behind.
Gone.
No going back.

Nothing exists *in front*.

Poem 6

We can never go back

Consciousness, empty and full.
Mind watches,
Ears listen,
Eyes see,
Skin feels.
Everything as it was, is and will ever be.

Mind at ease, still, conscious,
resting in the knowing
that it can never go back.
Never can it rebuild that salt doll.
Never can it re-animate that corpse.

Anxiety, panic, worry disappear
Never to arise again.

What is different now?

Mind rests in the bed of inevitability…

LIFE, DIVINITY, PERFECTION,
rejoicing that never has it to DO anything,
CONTROL anything,
EXPECT anything
anymore.

Free, free, free.

Poem 7

No separation

Yes

No judgement,
No preference,
No difference,
No separation,
No desire.

Mind knows this,
so why does the fight go on?

Last night ... anxiety like a schizophrenic.
Gecko jumped on God's behalf,
'Stop it!'

Slowly, slowly, sinking slowly,
deeper and deeper,
realising the inevitability
of every action.

Wake up, eyes open.
What will the day bring?
So, we just do it.
What?
Anything that presents itself.

With every step, the path unfolds.
Divinity manifests in
God's time.

Dying throes,
weaker and weaker.
Mind quietens.
Moments deepen.
Self loses its self

Actor and action meld.
No doer.
No separation.

Poem 8

Have you had enough, yet?

Such a relief ...
Not to have to do anything more.
Not to have to strive to be something.
Not to have know everything.
Not to have to chase my tail,
driven by the voice saying
'YOU ARE NOT GOOD ENOUGH!'

I don't have to learn this by next week.
I don't have to know that by next week.
I don't have to get a job yesterday.
I don't have to do anything.

Such a relief,
lying here not having to DO anything.

No desire to be anything,
anyone,
happy,
successful.

That mask was so heavy, so stressful.
Driven by...
not feeling good enough ...
EVER.

Utter desolation.
Some call it surrender.

I could sleep forever.

A lifetime of TRYING to be something I'm not.
Such weight,
Utter exhaustion.

Are you ready to let go now, MIND?
Have you had enough of thrashing?
Aren't you so TIRED?
Why do you keep trying? Fighting?
Do you still feel
NOT GOOD ENOUGH?
Have you let that go?

When you do, you can be free.
No desire left to drive the anxiety.

Have you had enough, yet?

Poem 9

Enough

Yes, yes, I have had ENOUGH!
Please let me be free.
I don't want to be in control.
I never had control.
The effort has left me MAD.

So mad I want to die.

I needed a job,
Needed to keep my skills up
or they would disappear,
and I would never be
GOOD ENOUGH.
What would people think?
My father suffered the same.
It killed him.

Ah Papa, let me finish this for us.

We have had enough.
We don't need to try anymore.
We can stop and rest.
We can enjoy every moment
without that torturous arrow
burning in our flank.
It has burnt itself out.

Finished. Enough.
No more samskaras feeding
desire.

The raging inferno has burnt itself out.

It's gone. Had ENOUGH.

You and I can be free now. Desireless.

3. My Dreams: What is Real?

2016 Dreams and Visions

My dreams and visions have always been vividly cinematic. Towards the end of 2015 and at the beginning of 2016, the dreaming intensified with additional nightly experiences leaving me exhausted and questioning my sanity. At the time of occurrence, these dreams and visions were tangible and real to my senses. Who knows what they were or what they signified. All I can say is that the experiences were transient and filtered through my mind. They are just another stepping-stone on the journey of this life …

Feb 7, 2016: Dream – While swimming in the ocean, a cat swam up to me and regurgitated a pearl as a gift for me.

Feb 9: Dream – I ended up stuck in a dark basement with Archangel Gabriel sitting on a couch explaining life to me.

Feb 13: Dream – I was flying, and a Ulysses butterfly was trying to guide me safely away from people.

Feb 16: Dream – Again, I was flying trying to get away from people.

Feb 17: Dream – I was driving a car down the steep range and then slid 90 degrees down a rock hill and landed on the bottom safely.

Feb 20: Dream – I was on a rocket ship going 'home', but had to divert to a distant station first.

Feb 21: Vision – I merged with my Self – a vision of myself floated in front of me, towards me and then into my body.

Feb 25: Dream – A Hyena and a tiger prostrated in front of me. The tiger tried to push the hyena away. I hugged the hyena and chastised the tiger.
Vision – I was deep asleep, but wide awake, conscious of myself sleeping and watching the creation of universes.

Feb 26: Dream – I was doing dentistry on a Sufi master.

Feb 28: Dream – I had nowhere to stay. Tried to get a hotel room, but it was too expensive. Ended up at the hotel buffet. A stranger in the food line grasped my shoulders, turned me around to face him and kissed me. My empty plate became full. Then I saw my father in the distance waiting for me.

Mar 1: Vision – I came face-to-face with my Self, who said to me, 'You are Me; I am You' three times.
Dream 1 – I had super powers, but superpowers were not ready to be used.
Dream 2 – I was told, 'You don't need to go to work, someone is substituting for you, just relax, a surprise is coming.'

Mar 3: Vision – I walked past and bowed to figures on the mountain – mountain Gods?

Mar 4: Dream – I was in a dark room and didn't want to disturb anyone or make noise. I felt a power inside me, but opted not to move glass, only metal. Used latent power to move metal. Saw the power working. Was amazed.

Mar 9: Vision – I woke up in the night and didn't know where I was.
Dream – I went to a bar, and the bartender (Narayan Maharaj – an Indian Master associated with Meher Baba) made me a special cocktails.

Mar 6: Dream 1 – three children were holding a huge hose and washing away all the people and the whole scene.
Dream 2 – I saw Mum walking alone. I ran up to her, so glad to see her (God). Prostrated myself down at her feet.
Dream 3 – I was travelling with two bags, both empty.

Mar 24: Vision – I woke up to a clanging noise. A red, fiery figure was floating in front of my eyes then merged into me. Twice. The second time I could see a female figure with many arms. She reminded me of the Indian Goddess Kali.

Apr 1: Vision 1 – I had that merging experience again. This time I merged with large Buddha eyes that floated towards me and then into me.
Vision 2 – more merging. I merged into an old Greek-looking man, and then a wild-looking man.
Vision 3 – I was floating, then approached a figure that looked like a an ancient Egyptian statue guarding a cave. Went through into the cave and floated up a tall stone tower with many levels up to the top level. Each level was a test. Finally, I got to go to the summit of the tower. As I floated upward, I found a mirror. When I looked into the mirror, I saw the reflection of an old

medicine man with my hair, a painted face and sharpened ferocious teeth.

Apr 9: Vision – I was asleep but awake all night with many figures from all eras, mainly Greek and Roman scholar types floating towards me and merging into me. One waved at me from on top of a Greek temple.

Apr 23: Dream 1 – I was at the beach and saw a dead clown fish and a dead turtle. In the distance, a bear emerged from the water. I was petrified. Tried to run. Couldn't move. Managed to fly clumsily away from the danger.
 Dream 2 – I had surgery on my tongue. Afterwards, I saw my own severed head on the counter waiting for healing.
Dream 3 – At home, a family came into the house, one diverted my attention while another stole cash from a wallet on the counter and denied it.

Apr 26: Dream 1 – I was trying to move very heavy luggage.
Dream 2 – I was trying to find a bus route home.
Dream 3 – Mum and I were fostering a baby; we lifted up a skin flap on its forehead to reveal two normal eyes plus five extra forehead eyes. We were reluctant to adopt the baby permanently.

Apr 27: Dream – Everyone in the meditation group and my family left me alone at a restaurant.

Apr 28: Dream – I was not included and left alone at meal time.

May 1: Dream 1 – I broke out of jail, but let the old man next to me go instead because I was already free.

Dream 2 – I was arrested to go to jail for a year but never went to jail. Tried to phone Mum but couldn't get through.

Oct 19: Vision – Meher Baba (elderly) approached me from the left side and gently touched my hand and then did the same on the right side, and then walked in front of me and gave me a kiss on the forehead.

Discourse with the self about dreams: Aug 5, 2016

This morning I woke up into a *dream*, yesterday it was *real*. So when I fall asleep and dream, is that a dream? Or when I wake up, am I waking from reality into a dream? What is real?

When my hand is cut, pain is felt. Is that real? When my eyes open and see the ceiling, is that real?

If there is no me, then what is looking at the ceiling? Who is looking at the ceiling? Who feels the pain when my hand is cut?

In this dream, who creates the dream?

> *Analysis of the question*
> *Centre* (the *one*, the *real*) ——> projection of the one = manifestation = existence

The *one* = What Meher Baba calls <u>Beyond the beyond</u> = Pure ISness = **Centre** of the black hole where infinity compresses into nothing (my words).

There is Beyond the beyond; it lies beyond the mind, beyond consciousness. Then 'closer' to mind, there is the beyond. 'Beyond' is beyond the mind, but within consciousness and can be said to be 'separate' from Beyond the beyond for ease of understanding. Beyond is the projection of the 'Beyond the beyond'. If visualised linearly, it lies between the **centre** and the mind. The beyond is not real, it is a projection.

Beyond the beyond is the centre. The beyond is the projection of the centre, the source of existence and by nature, *unmanifest*.

The projection (the beyond) uses *pure mind* as a tool for the *manifestation* of existence. The projection of the *real centre*, cannot manifest without *pure mind*. *Mind* is the vehicle of manifestation of *existence*.

*Mind = pure mind = mind without identity, without ego. Where the clearest reflection can be seen of what is *real* (but it not truly real as it is still only the projection of the *real*).

*mind = identified mind = a mind with an identity and an ego garment = ego-mind complex = small self.

Manifestation begins as pure energy – particles of potential. This is similar to the light that shines into the projector to produce an image on the screen. Mind is the screen, manifestation is the energy that lights up and becomes the image on the screen. Existence is the image on the screen.

If the screen is pure and clean, it is a perfect mirror reflecting the truest image of the *real*. If the screen is tainted by *ego* and cloaked by identity, the image will be what the ego wants, separate from the *real*.

Centre is infinity – empty, dark, black hole, nothingness (Beyond, beyond the mind)

Projection of the centre – energy, light (it lies beyond the mind) - unmanifest existence.

Pure mind – screen on which *existence* can be perceived as it truly is. The vehicle for manifestation.

Existence – the image on the screen of *pure mind*.

Ego-mind – screen on which an ego-created *illusory* existence can be perceived; a vehicle of the ego to define a false self and avoid its annihilation.

Illusion – the image on the screen of the small mind created by the ego-self.

*

So what happens when we sleep?

Pure mind goes back to the source, the centre; mind keeps itself and the screenplay active with *dreaming*.

When we open our eyes in the morning, we activate the mind through the senses becoming a part of the image on the screen.

If the ego-mind is present, the screen is covered by thoughts coming from the ego projecting on the screen of the mind. Here the mind and ego are cloaked in identity; they have become synonymous with the small 'I' (the ego-mind complex) and have becomes rulers of their own kingdom. The ego-mind usurps the screen, covering the truth underneath a cloak of fabricated illusion (thoughts).

By nature, the ego-mind is completely oblivious to what lies under the cloak. The *real* is hidden from view. The ego-mind defines the self and falls under the spell of its own illusion. The ego uses the mind to crystallise its own imaginary identity and avoid the annihilation of its self-made, self-perpetuating false self. The ego-mind is an illusion and through itself, it creates further illusion – an illusion within an illusion.

If our small ego-mind is present, our existence becomes the illusion of the mind, where our ego-mind is the boss.

If our ego-mind has realised its illusory nature, it disappears and our existence is a reflection of the *real* – this is who we really are.

So, to answer the introductory questions:
Is the pain real?
No.

Is the ceiling real?
No.

Is all a dream or a dream within a dream?
Yes.

Who creates the dream?
- Ego-mind – if the eyes are perceiving through a tainted screen of ego-mind, the image is completely false
- *Pure mind* – if the eyes are perceiving through a mirror-like, pure screen of the *pure mind*, the image is true

Who is looking at the wall?
- Either the small self (the created ego-mind)
- Or the *one* who is looking through the *pure mind* – this must be the *centre* looking from the Beyond the beyond?

Everything comes from the centre – Beyond the beyond

Our perpetual journey is—————-> from centre out then back into centre.

Note 1: Words are so inadequate at conveying all this, but it's all I have.

Note 2: This essay is written through a mind. The beyond cannot be known except through experience. When the ego-mind has evaporated, *pure mind* is left to experience itself...of that I cannot speak as I don't know with any certainty at this point.

Discourse with the self – Aug 6, 2016

The black hole, this is who I AM.

Part 2: Seeking in Earnest

4. Dark Night of the Soul: Journal Sept 2017–Mar 2018

Sept 19, 2017

More pain

What the hell do I know?

Life is hell, it hurts.

I hate everyone! It hurts to be around anyone. Just get me out of here. End it now please.

There is no God, so who is there to turn to? No-one

Not even my mother. There is *NO-ONE*.

Fuck work ... forget everyone. I hate it all. Please let it end. End, end, end.

Words, words, words. That's all it ever was. The experience behind it is NULL! Fake!

Pain, pain, pain!

Let the eternal slumber come please.

So what if this is mind? It is all that can be seen now. If it is mind, it has nothing to do with me. I can't control it; I can't control anything. Every action HURTS. I can't do anything without feeling pain.

Please bring sleep that I don't have to wake up from. Oh, it's always about me, me, me – fuck it all!

There's nothing left for me to give, so what more can be given? What is all this pain for? YOU (God, universe, whatever?) already have ALL of me, so what more is there to take?

*

Later in the day ...

Reading Meher Baba and Milarepa gave me fleeting moments of peace. That's it. It's not real; it doesn't last. No-one can help. No-one can hear. No-one is there, just me.

Just me ... as it always was and will be. So tired, so tired. Time to sleep. Please. How?

There's no choice but to allow these thoughts to come up. What choice is there? None.

This body aches, and this mind is in pain. It all hurts. It's ALL suffering. I don't know anything else anymore. I can't see beyond me. It feels like being trapped in a tiny bubble. Painful.

Too many words pass through this small mind and get lost in a maze. They don't mean anything.

Why do I have such resistance to going to work? It's so hard to be there when I'm not there. It's so hard when I'm forced to be somewhere all the time and concentrate all day listening to people who expect you to fix them flawlessly. Arrgh, other people's expectations. I hate living up to other people's expectations. I don't have to do shit! So what? They can all get fucked!

Time is getting closer. Dread sets in. I don't understand why it's always this way. I have such dread of not living up to an expectation. But, isn't God is the doer? What a bunch of shit when I don't experience that directly!

Fuck it and you all! Obliterate this existence. Haven't I experienced enough? How many times do I have to go through the suffering to know myself? How many? It's like a childish game. Why do I do it? Why? It's masochistic self-suffering. I already know!

I give up, please. The end is nigh. Why get up? More suffering. No, thank you!

Sept 20, 2017

Fear of death

Why work? To make money. To live.

Why worry? Because of the fear of not enough shelter, food, comfort?

Let the body die then. Then the fear of the body's death won't run the show.

I give up, please.

The end must be nigh.

Why get up? More suffering.

No thank you!

Sept 27, 2017

Nothing

Nothing remains. No time, nothing to do, no past, no future. Just the *now*, however it comes.

Today my body aches; my mind fuzzes. So I'm just lying here writing this.

Life is a surreal dream, sometimes noisy and chaotic, sometimes tranquil, sometimes flowing easily, sometimes challenging physically or mentally.

People, in general, don't mean anything, but when they are within proximity, they mean everything.

No more Pollyanna, no more urge to do-good, fix people, make them right, rescue their suffering. It's not my job; there is no 'my' anything.

Nothing to live up to.

Don't have to do it right.

Don't have to do anything at all.

Anything is possible.

Nothing can be lost.

Life cannot be lost.

The linear path infinitely expands into many dimensions and then overrides the senses. Metaphorically 'riding the *divine wave*' is maybe more understandable as a verb. More like *being* the *divine wave*.

It is not understandable or graspable by the mind.

I don't even know what to write about. Words cannot describe what I feel or want to express.

I can't read books, can't watch stuff, can't do anything except act on inspiration.

Nov 15, 2017

Wisp 1

Last thread lingering forever. Can it be let go just like that?

Must it play out?

Does the illusory mind need to have resolution to move beyond itself?

If mind is not real (but an illusory tool for awareness to use), the self is not real and nothing can be done.

So can the mind-state, knowing this, just let it go?

Yes.

The blockage to freedom is imagined. So what is attempting to hold on? That pesky thread of nothing interpreted as 'I'm not good enough', the identity on which this created mind has used to perpetuate itself. It's as if this mind were based upon the striving for perfection and a constant state of worry.

The mind wants something, anything, to worry about then it has tangibility and it can feel itself. Ha ha.

Every moment is new, so how can tomorrow be predicted? It can only be projected based on nothing.

This physical vehicle breathes, eats, moves, sleeps ... what animated it in the first place? What moves through it? Is the body even real?

Nov 15, 2017

Wisp 2

So, in my case, life so far has been playing out the samskara of pleasing others and making up for being 'not good enough'. This translates into a Pollyanna, a perfectionist worrier. Archetypal and so annoying. My poor mum!

So, what was the infernal thread that has been coming up and causing me extreme anxiety in relation to work? Simply put, it was based upon the combination of the need to make people happy and the feeling of not being good enough. Daily angst, nightly worry, constant torture, and the mind lapped it up with glee! It was all such juicy fodder for the mind to sink its teeth into. So much was the suffering that the mind was forced to turn inward or end its physical existence. Those were the only choices.

All that remains of those threads is a subtle light mist veiling here from there. Ha ha. But since the revelation about my life tonight, that veil has lifted, seemingly. Wait, let me check ...

Yep. First, the mind has recognised that it is not real and is just a state (mind-state), as Mum said, like a sixth sense – eyes, ears, nose, mouth, skin and mind (perception).

Yep, I can feel vestiges of the wisp, but the associated anxiety or fodder for the 'mind' is gone.

Yippppppeeee!

So what now? What happens when the awareness is pure, unmasked by any memory or samskara? Every moment is new, fresh, unknown, an utter mystery, the ultimate adventure, completely *free*.

I shall have to see about that.

More on the wisps, aka the remnants of the onion after it is peeled. The samskara is gone, but the smell remains in the mind until it has played out on the physical level (which could be a long time) or the mind sees it for what it is and just *lets go*.

Awareness can only get stronger, thicker, denser, concentrated, more pervading, more and more infinite.

Awareness – mind-state not engaged, infinite, no time.

Mind-state – mind-state engaged, concentration, finite, time (functional).

Nov 19, 2017

Flick the switch ...

... Nothing. The mind is totally blank. Expansion. Then focus on the screen to write about it.

Went to lunch with friends today. Sat in silence, then noticed that they were sitting in silence too. We all sat together quietly in that space.

Really, there isn't much to say about it.

There is mind, and then there is no mind ... and the awareness that follows. What lies in between is the illusory terrain that each mind has to traverse and spends lifetimes doing so.

How can this be communicated to anyone who searches for an answer? They already think they know because their mind dictates. But then they feel that 'this' is not it, nether is 'that'nor 'that'. It is a process of elimination until nothing remains.

If this body is here just to experience and live until it sheds its gross form, so be it. If there is any sort of communicating to be done about the matter, then it seems most effectively done in silence or anonymity. Leave the machinations of the mind to the masters of the mind as it is exhausting, torturous work.

There is a process occurring on all levels. In addition to the described experiences, my body has been inspired to strengthen from the inside out. Re-arranging and renewing seems to be occurring. Preparations for what is to come, no doubt.

Nov 19, 2017

Finding the words ...

Over the past years and months, I've read all the accounts and words of past 'masters', but none have described what is happening to me now. Krishnamurti has come the closest. Osho, who has been such a soothing companion over the last six months, now sounds like a self-aggrandising prattler. The dearest Meher Baba has disintegrated into the past. My experience at Avatar's Abode (I went on a trip to Meher Baba's Queensland sanctuary) was truly a reflection of the end of the 'guru' era – the 'dying' was palpable.

So what now?

People have used the words God-realisation, enlightenment, nirvakalpa samadhi, etc. No words can be used. Once they are, the mind has reinforced the illusion of itself in a different way.

What can be said? Just what is the purpose of this shell of a body breathing and interacting? There is no answer forthcoming at the moment for these questions. Maybe the answers will come ... or not. Or maybe 'knowing' the answer perpetuates illusion.

*

Description of my mind-state now: When the mind-state has no focus, the shell/persona/entity/gross body just sits still in awareness. In this awareness there is overlying perception – ears hear, eyes see, nose smells, skin feels, consciousness receives (like a satellite). The feeling is of expansion and contraction.

When things are to be done, the body does them, when people come into the physical sphere, the senses focus. Activities arise, but none are sought.

Occasionally, and more frequently these days, the senses are very sensitive, and sound, especially, reverberates through the head.

Tiredness comes very heavily in the early hours of the evening. Waking occurs early (on sunrise), without ability to 'fall back asleep'. Some days in my waking state, focusing is more difficult and tiring.

Funnily though, once at 'work' and forced to be focused, actions come easily. Once work finishes, the 'tiredness' again descends very quickly and heavily.

Who knows what this is? I have not read any description of what I am currently experiencing. I know nothing of Krishnamurti's experiences of feeling like the 'entire universe'.

It feels like the shell surrounding my Self has been emptying and, no doubt, will keep emptying infinitely, if that is possible. As it empties, it becomes more infinite. Can infinity keep growing?

Is there any fear in me?

I'm not sure.

Not to negate any others' words, but (for me) there has never been any experience of:

'Everything is God.'

'I am God.'

'God is real.'

'Everything is love.'

'Overflowing bliss.'

So this new awareness does not feel good or bad.

When in a group, it is most comfortable sitting quietly still while listening and reacting naturally ... or being up and about, doing what needs to be done. Trying to fit into general group conversation goes completely 'against the grain' and is much too difficult at the moment.

Anything that is too 'difficult' does not occur. It happens in sync or it does not happen at all. In other words, 'too hard basket' is not acted upon. The end result is of no consequence.

When I look out at nature, it elicits a quicker, expansive experience within my being, but it is not perceived the way Krishnamurti describes in his notebook – like an amazing, unique experience. Certain environments, actions and people elicit this expansion. Others force focus. Expansion seems like the natural state and focusing seems like more of a conscious effort. Maybe because the mind-state needs to be activated?

My natural state is expansive, senses aware, but not engaged, mind-state inactive; Mum calls it awareness.

A visual description of this awareness: gross objects blend and reduce to their energy state, and separateness of objects blurs into a matrix of homogenous pattern.

What causes the matrix to crystallise and become separate objects?

*

Saying 'I' is a way of referring to the shell. So stupid trying to avoid saying 'I', 'me' or 'my' as it sounds silly and manufactured. But I have to clarify that those words do not feel like they are referring to a self, anymore. Guess that might sound strange to most.

Nov 19

More blah, blah ...

I'm lying here with the computer at my fingertips testing what will happen ...

Is there such thing as truth? The truth? How can one know? Truth for any one person is entirely encapsulated within their own experience. That is all. There is no single definition of the truth, at least not one that can be defined by words.

There is a restlessness pervading me today. Something imminent, expectant, a sense of unsettledness. Transitionary angst.

No thoughts enter the mind-state.

Reading back on these words that are written, I realise that the meaning of the words is secondary to the experience that the words elicit for the reader. It's the same with every esoteric, spiritual book that has ever been written. The most important factor in writing is the experience of the writer. This experience filters through to the reader in some way. This is what the reader receives as the greatest gift from the writer. It follows to say that when an original text is edited or altered, there is a danger of diluting the original experience.

Who will ever read these words? Will they understand what I mean? The knowledge imparted by the words do not matter in the end as the energy behind the words will transmit to the reader. All the knowledge gained from years of reading spiritual texts – Lord Meher's biography, Krishnamurti's words, etc – has gone, but the deep resonance and experience of the energies gained while reading have done their work over the years. Of course, they served to get my mind to this point in time.

Throughout history, aware individuals have lived, taught and passed on their wisdom through the spoken and written words. They come and they go, and their words are immortalised on paper and recorded on video. Yet the world continues to teeter on the brink of total unconsciousness, lost in materialism and self-focus.

In other words, there is a cycle, an ebb and flow of human consciousness rising and falling. This gross world of form living within the limitations of time is the battleground of the mind and is a necessary journey. Within the hologram of time, the spectrum of awareness spans from unconscious to conscious to aware – with a large expanse between each.

Within duality, there is always a battle. Who can step out of it? Only a very few? Even those who recognise their unconsciousness cannot readily step off the treadmill. Those few who move beyond duality maintain balance and clear the 'way' for others to find their way through, too.

Nov 19 cont'd

There is absolutely nothing to do. I'm just lying here experiencing doing nothing. The most difficult part is not falling asleep (or wherever the awareness goes when the mind is consciously gone).

There's no bliss, no God, no nothing.

But there is no separation either.

Nor is there fear, past, future, love, attachment, disappointment.

The space that enveloped us today at lunch is always here. It envelops everything around it. Anything that comes into our proximity or focus will get caught up in that space.

Why do I work with people? To share that space. Everything else is incidental. It doesn't really matter what is done for our daily 'work'. It can be anything that elicits proximity to or focus upon the space.

This writing is so out there, it is only for clarification of the awareness.

We eat food, exercise and take care of the body as a vehicle for the state that it can share.

There is no sense of urgency. It has always been, always will be and is always now.

If there really is a hierarchy of aware beings, I have no idea or conception of it. I only can share the process that I have been going through as an example of the implosion of the mind. I have not found any books or versions explaining clearly what this process is or how it proceeds from here. Everything available is only written in mind language. Following the implosion, it is all experiential, and I may not be able to impart it with words. But I'll try.

Blah, blah. Boring myself.

What do you want to ask? Or know?

Nov 21, 2017

Bag of impressions

There is absolutely nothing in the mind. I'm just lying here in fasting mode. My body is not uncomfortable, but a bit extra spacey. It's almost in dormant mode, ready for anything to happen. Every moment is a great adventure!

Yesterday seemed to dissipate some anxiety in my mind. It's adventure time now ...

*

Stream of words ...

The grandeur and largess of life lies within the miracle of the moment. (Who is talking?) Words bombard the senses and attempt to capture the attention and obsession of the mind. The interplay between individual consciousness unfolds as interactions have been predesigned according to the need for certain tendencies to be brought forth and experienced. And released ... or not. The change is always there for one to release latent impressions. If not released, they are stored back in the 'bag' of the mind to arise another time.

People, words and activities that enter one's field become the greatest opportunities for absolution from suffering. Yet these chances are not much realised.

Once free of impressions, ultimate freedom and pure awareness reveal the miracle of life.

But it is not fair to talk of such a state too much.

The simple fact is that there is a choice at every moment to let go or hold on. This determines the weight of one's 'bag of impressions'. The weight of the world lies within that bag causing all the suffering and emotions borne out of suffering.

One can never try to release themselves from the weight as such trying only makes the bag heavier.

So within the moments of sharing, if one or both of the sharers are sitting in awareness, the bag gets lighter. Spontaneous release, maybe?

As the day comes to a close, more is revealed every moment, yet it passes like clouds never to be reconstructed. Memories fade quickly.

The fasting has not been difficult. Surprisingly, attachment to food has also emptied out. Eating and the ritual surrounding planning, preparation and enactment of meals takes up so much time and energy. Surprisingly so. Food is a huge filler of space and consciousness, thus the food obsession for those looking for something they can't find.

Nov 24, 2017

Exhaustion

Last night, I dreamed all night of apocalyptic events where Mum and I (in one dream) were waiting for the huge cataclysm that would kill us all. We waited calmly in a bunker as if nothing was wrong. Dream after dream had the same theme of impending death, but I was not perturbed in the least. I was completely calm. But woke up exhausted.

This is a bizarre phenomenon really. I have been waking up 'exhausted' for a few days now – that is what it feels like, except that as soon as something has to be done, the feeling disappears and the action is easy to complete. Once the action is complete, the 'exhaustion' returns. Tonight was the worst when I was driving back from work in a trance and unable to do anything.

I can easily focus my attention, but getting up to do certain things is virtually impossible. Weird!

'Exhausted' could also be described as very out of it or spacey. Noises and people hurt my sensibilities right now.

Nov 26, 2017

Anticipation

It has been a few days since the 'exhausting day' (Nov 24th) where function seemed impossible.

Since then the days have been easier, interestingly simple, but very different, too.

Picked an Osho card tonight: Completion.

Maybe a completion is what it was all about? Dreams fill my night sky – strange dreams and faraway people – more emptying, most likely. Mum did mention something in the astrological line-up that suggested a time of purification.

It's hard to explain. These are easy days. No effort. No anxiety. There is an underlying current of expectancy as I wait for the ushering of a new era. It will be interesting to see how this manifests on the physical plane.

Sleep is a strange event. For weeks and months, fatigue would hit me at nightly at about 8 p.m. Since Nov 24th, there has been no fatigue like this, but I can still fall asleep quite easily (although sleep has been filled with dreams).

I can't read or watch shows, so have been listening to music. I have been inspired to go to great lengths to attend the ballet/pilates classes that my being just loves on all levels! My body is changing, getting stronger. Sweet foods repel my taste buds – yuck!

The feeling of impending change is so strong. Every moment is filled with anticipation.

Nov 29, 2017

Unsettled

Unsettled ... that's a word for you.

Grumpy, opinionated and not-so-nice – those are more words that describe me today.

Ever since the exhausted day (maybe a completion), the spaciness has subsided. Maybe because that spaciness is now becoming a 'normal' state of consciousness.

There's a sense of detachment from all around me, especially from the dog. Bizarre. There is also an urge within to get rid of everything old and unused. Have given away books, cleaned out clothes and all the cupboards.

Also – random fact – did my first full sit up yesterday. It seemed so easy after being so hard. What a very strange phenomenon.

Who is this persona? It seems stripped of old impressions and any wisps of remaining garments.

I have no idea. Mum mentioned something about the mind's inertia playing out. Maybe so.

It feels a bit negative; I don't feel nice or that comfortable in this skin at the moment.

Hmm – it's all transient. Nothing ever stays the same, even from day to day.

Nov 30, 2017

More anxiety

Life always brings what we need to dig out the latent weeds burrowed beneath the surface.

My mind is again holding off an onslaught of anxiety. Instead of relaxing and accepting, it tries to gain a foothold of control.

Attachments are severed one by one. Just when one feels completely detached, life acts on the stage to showcase another attachment that must be dissolved.

Attachment to keeping my mother safe is a big one. So is the feeling of security in a so-called 'home' environment. No such thing! The only place we can feel safe in is the place that has no security (obviously, that is what my mind is saying).

Dec 10, 2017

Spacey

These days are indescribable. I'm just floating along with no purpose except whatever is in the moment. Every moment is acting on the stage to bring me deeper into myself and weed out any impression that stands in the way of clarity.

Last night was tinged with anxiety. The mind-state was trying to push through and engulf my persona with fear. Only awareness and complete acceptance of this occurrence allowed it to subside and 'stare through the glass barrier', but not get through. I still feel detached from all.

The spacey state must have become the norm. It isn't as pronounced as before.

Listening to Osho's ramblings ... he did have a strong self that needed protection and cutting humour to defend. He talks of enlightenment like he knows all about it, yet he defends his mind-self strongly, so the dichotomy remained in his life.

What to do? Just play it out as it comes.

The world contains such extremes of dichotomy – such abhorrent cruelty and base animal urges, and such kindness and compassion. Both bring us to our knees, wondering why it all has to be. Such suffering – on one hand, the ones who cause the suffering and, on the other, the ones who suffer so greatly. This must accelerate the enlightenment process greatly. Each side has to flip, and both are experienced by the one. Both lead to the great, infinite step inward.

How do I feel?

I can't say that I feel the perfection, bliss, peace, but I know that everything is perfect and nothing need be changed. The instant my mind-state is out out of the present and into the past or future, the suffering begins – future as anxiety; past as depression or regret.

So crazy.

I am writing these words – maybe for no-one, maybe for someone or maybe for many to come. The process is my own, thus this writing is a bunch of words that anyone can interpret according to their own experience. Their process will be their own. Do not pay too much attention to my process.

Actually, nothing that I have written will probably appeal to anyone. There has been no glory, no bliss, no lightning strike of clarity. Though it can be said that the recent all-consuming anxiety is virtually non-existent, there is no loneliness, no hurt feelings, no suffering as there used to be. Just a benign floating along right now.

All spirituality has faded away. I'm not reading any of the books anymore. Meher Baba is gone, Krishnamurti gone, Osho gone. No master remains. No-one remains. No face remains. There is no-one to turn to.

Dec 11, 2017

Life is very simple. There is nothing to it except this moment.

Jan 1, 2018

Pathetic and self-absorbed.

Jan 3, 2018

Alien

Day after day passes and words get scarcer and scarcer.

Christmas was very relaxing. The feeling of alienation seeped through me as all the people socialised and met new friends. I have nothing to say and no motivation to be out there socialising as I once was. That social creature was a facade that has faded into oblivion. She is gone – the nice, caring, social, chatty, friendly person. Who is left? Hmmm.

The feeling of alien-ness reached a climax at New Year's dinner with family and familiar faces. I felt like an alien in a strange land that used to be familiar. Mum says this is the mind judging the emptiness as 'alien-ness' and in a negative fashion.

Not much remains, not even a smile. The mind is quite blank, really.

My appetite has diminished for most things. Sleep brings relief to a decimated space that used to be 'mind'.

Work passed by with no worries, no sense of time or urgency.

Mum says now to remain 100% in the moment aware of life and its gifts.

Jan 5, 2018

Tortured mind

Implosion.

This is not my body; there is no feeling of privilege to be in a body, regardless of what all the spiritual books say. I would happily drop this body at any time.

There is no reason to be, no-one to serve, no-one to take care of, no reason to eat or breathe ...

There's even no reason to go to work; why go with days like these? The existing employees can take up the slack easily. There is no special path.

My family seems alien to me. My raison d'être all along has been taking care of Mum. She is taken care of; she has her carer. Her body seems like a burden to her on all levels. At all levels Mum's body has been of service.

I can't even cry right now.

Will there be inspiration about where to go and what to do next? I'm feeling like a Mast (one consumed by the Divine,) like this consciousness could lose itself as these ties that are keeping it here and 'normal' fade away.

The threads are thinning; the forces keeping me here are losing the battle.

I feel no connection to anyone and a burden to my mother – my master teacher.

I can't even be upset. There is no hiding; I'm just not needed or wanted anywhere or by anyone. Is being needed or wanted a reason for existence?

Maybe my body and mind belong in a nuthouse?

My grasp on life is tenuous. I'm losing the impetus to get up and live. There is no reason, but life has continued until now. Now everything has *stopped*.

Without Mum, my body would be long gone by now.

It's funny. I'm not hungry, but then have eaten just enough today to sustain the body. The mind is not hungry.

All the spiritual pundits say that this body is a gift. To be on earth in a human body is a great privilege.' Blah, blah and all that nonsense.

When Mum is no longer, no-one left will see me. Then my invisibility will be 100%.

Seemingly, every action of mine is to serve people – calling them, cooking for them ...

Jan 28, 2018

Hormones

There's nothing, nothing at all

The 'emptiness' in my mind must be getting larger. I have pressure in my head, coupled with physical hormones (PMT) and an impending blue moon + eclipse, which makes for a frantic time. Today, the underlying sense of unease has subsided but still meanders in the background.

In the last few days since the electricity blowout, installation of the new internet connection and purchase of a new computer, my energy has been haywire – tired and wired as sleep is lacking, too. It's like being caffeinated without the caffeine intake. I'm sleeping late, bored and wake up early – a cortisol feeling.

Mum and I finished dismantling the kitchen yesterday. Both of us were so exhausted we could barely talk. During exercise class yesterday, it felt like my head was going to blow off. My face was red and so hot. High blood pressure maybe? Or an energy thing?

Today I'm trying to relax before the impending five-day work week. The mind looks forward to the days off, but while lying around reading, I can't help but feel like something should be happening.

Hopefully, this is not the reason that the mind is trying to find a new project.

Current mind interpretation of the 'emptiness': unease, pressure in the head, speediness.

Mar 3, 2018

Flying

It's been a while. I've not much inkling to 'say' more with words.

This morning was the best dream so far: I was strolling and decided that I would fly for no reason at all (usually it happens running away from something I am afraid of and struggling, always trying to hide the flying from people's eyes). So I made the decision to fly and took off, but saw the ceiling in front of me. Usually I would try and fly around it, but it posed no barrier. It was not real. So I just flew straight through it. The flight became faster and faster, freer and freer, going with the flow – completely and utterly free. I felt the wind rushing by as I flew out of the earth's atmosphere into the cosmos and empty space. As I was revelling in the freedom and flow, suddenly there was no *me* left. Then my fingers started to move like I was playing the piano (but I don't know how to play the piano). The no *me* became someone else who played the piano. Then I became someone else and ended up in some room ...

The alarm went off at that point.

Over breakfast, Mum said, 'Now, don't go back to the old mind patterns.'

Mar 6, 2018

Pressure

Agony**

'I' would like to die.

Please, please, stop this.

The pressure crushes my head. Just please let go. There is such bondage of responsibility.

Please, please.

The pressure, negativity, urge to self-destruct is taking over. My head just needs to explode, then all will be clear.

I can't do it anymore. This life. I can disappear. It would be a relief.

**There was nothing else to do but allow the agony to play itself out. Like all things, it came to an end.

Mar 8, 2018

Rainbow

Amazing rainbow.

I woke up with the same bereft feeling. Mum reminded me of what is real. The mind's duality and need for judgement of negative or positive is not real.

Driving to work, the most amazing rainbow greeted me. A triple rainbow. So vivid and a complete full half. A second and then a third. It took my breath away and reduced me to tears.

Mar 15, 2018

Dreams

Last night was a doozy.

The night was filled with dreaming, visions and lucid sleep.

Dream, dream, dream. I'm trying to recall the details…

That's right, I had a realisation while sleeping: The emptiness and the fullness are *one* and do not manifest without each other. In duality, they are represented by the female and male. Yin and yang. Lock and key.

Part 3: Nirvana

5. The Turning Point

Mar 19, 2018

Everything changed from this day

Catalyst.

It was an insignificant workday, which ended with an insignificant event triggering a fury within that overcame me as I drove home.

So much anger and rebellion rose up against 'my' lack of control in life – fuck everything, fuck them all!

I yelled, screamed in the car, gave a truck the finger, then cried ...

Was this another karmic weed being ripped out and released? The weed of caring about people, wanting to dictate how people should be, feeling the pressure to make a certain amount of money every day, of not being worthy because everyone is busier and more successful than 'I' 'I' 'I'!

Note: On this day, the mind finally had enough of struggling. *Truly.* It just gave up and the illusion of self was annihilated. From this day on, the lifelong feeling of emptiness, desolation, separateness and suffering disappeared.

Mar 20, 2018

Another flying dream

I was lucid dreaming of sorts. In the dream, I made a conscious decision to fly (usually it happens spontaneously, as a reflex) and took off flying so *high* and *free*, faster than light, through the universe and cosmos. Stars flew by me. Then I made another choice to continue into the unknown, beyond any place I'd been before. A brief flash of fear surged through me of leaving the familiar and maybe not returning. But the fear disappeared as fast as it arose. The flying continued beyond the cosmos, the universe, beyond the known boundaries. Unimaginable freedom, stillness and movement. Flying with no restriction, no should's or have to's. Just complete *liberation*. Indescribable.

Hmm. Liberation. What from? Of mind from all illusion of any boundaries? Amazing.

The end of the dream was a haze. A bedroom. No-one around. The doona cover was the baby blue one from home with small white flowers. The same, but made of a different fabric. A parallel universe?

I woke up into this reality feeling empty after being wrenched away from the incredible feeling of liberation in the dream.

My feeling throughout the day was different, not in a negative sense, but it was a feeling of not caring what happened at all. Work had its 'challenges', which really weren't challenges at all because there was no sense of how things should be! Is that a taste of liberation in itself?

Mar 21, 2018

Resignation

Feeling the space.

So today was spent at home with Mum, just sitting, not doing anything at all. Consciously not doing things that the mind deems necessary i.e. weeding the garden, moving furniture, cleaning dust.

So here it is ... the state of 'not caring' but caring without attachment to outcome. Is this what Mum was talking about when she told me time and time again not to be attached to the outcome of any actions?

I was sitting in the *void*, accepting the *void*. There is 'not even a self left to be able to leave this place.' All the thoughts of not-wanting-to-be-here are nullified because there is not a self left to not want to be here.

Is this complete acceptance? The state of utter resignation such that the mind is beyond caring what happens *at all*?

It's not a state of glory and peace, but a state of *utter resignation*, left with *no choice at all*, but to be *here*. A state stripped of everything, naked, alone, desolate, *bereft*. Maybe this is like the final stages of someone terminally ill who knows death is imminent and accepts this *completely*.

Not sure if this 'process' is complete, but it's certainly happening at light speed!

Mar 22, 2018

A brand new day

I woke up with a sensation of great, rapid movement, like being in a moving vehicle. I had to try to recall where the body was and open my eyes slowly to capture the moment.

My awareness seems to be free from the shackles of mental machinations and creations. There is a liberation, of sorts, from any have-to-do's. Work, the greatest 'thorn-in-the-side' from the mind's point of view, has become not work, but something else to be done for the moment. The mind is nothing but a point of view dictating should, would, could and has-to-be's, which have nothing to do with what is.

I feel detached yet caring, but am not attached to the outcome – this is the only way to describe it. Driving (the usual daily route) was fresh and new, like off to a new adventure. I was just going to work, with no goals in mind, no aim for the day and no money to have to make. I felt no need to do anything, be anyone or have anything.

Is this a liberation of sorts?

The other day's meltdown on March 19th maybe was *the* meltdown. The 'mind' *really* had had enough and had finally taken its rightful place in a state of illusion.

I'm just visiting Earth and this body. Just visiting. This too shall pass ...

After years of seeking, Buddha finally gave up, knowing there was nothing more he could do. That night he became enlightened.

Mar 24, 2018

Another new day

Life is different now. A shift, maybe *the* shift is occurring.

Every moment is new and accepted as it is. Laughingly so.

The day brought pouring torrential rain this morning, drenched roads – some would call them treacherous – but oh-so-fun. I drove home, laughing and crying. For what reason, who knows? An image of the laughing Buddha came to mind. Laughing at the seriousness of it all and crying at the needless suffering.

Oh, hooray, hopefully ... it remains to be seen.

Exercise is done, food is bought, dog is content, stomach seems satisfied. All is well.

Mar 25, 2018

Samadhi, the movie

I watched *Samadhi*, the movie Part 1. Here are some snippets:

Attainment = mind. As long as one feels the need to attain something, the mind rules reality.

*

Before enlightenment, we push a rock uphill, after enlightenment, we also push a rock uphill, except something has changed – **the inner resistance disappears.** The struggle ceases. Or the one who struggles has been realised to be illusory and no longer exists. The individual will and higher mind are aligned. There is a dropping of all inner resistance to all phenomena so that inner freedom is not contingent upon the outer.

*

Enlightenment means being free to act without being driven by unconscious motives; it is acting in alignment with *life* not against it.

*

Where there is peace, there is also chaos. Out there and in here. Duality.

Within the mind, there is always a problem that needs solving. Beyond the mind, we are free of perspective and free to create new perspectives with no self-motivation.

*

Who am 'I' without my thoughts?

*

The day continued ...

I have an urge to write, thus clarifying this realisation that the *Samadhi* movie states so succinctly. I have watched the movie a few times and every time, my ears hear something different according to where my mind is at.

I have been trying to describe what has happened over the last week since the day of upheaval on March 19th, which was triggered by something insignificant (truly less than a speck of dust). This was the day of *enough*, when so much anger and rebellion erupted, and then I had the profound sense of, ' I don't give a #@*& what happens anymore!'

Does my experience echo the story of Buddha? After years of searching, he also finally gave up knowing there was nothing more he could do. Then he was liberated or enlightened.

Just a subtle, yet cataclysmic shift of perspective.

That day did not feel like a giving up, but rather the mind's volcanic reaction to its lack of control after trying so hard to do everything right. The volcanic eruption must have disintegrated the remnants of self ... and the mind just gave up. Just like that.

Then there was the dream of flying so free into the cosmos and beyond the known universe. So vast, so free, no boundaries!

Ever since, on this plane of awareness, I have had a sense of freedom from caring. It was so subtle at first – the words 'don't care' or 'not caring' come to mind, but they imply a lack of presence which is not the case. The state is more like complete presence in every moment without any investment in the outcome.

It can be likened to giving up everything: the need to succeed; the need to make money; the need to have people like and accept me; the need to have purpose.

So then, my mind tries to test this out by saying, 'Imagine life without Mum, then how would you be?'

Mum isn't here now, she is on holidays in Europe and there is no bereftness. But, what if she were gone forever? It is difficult to extrapolate a fictional situation. All is as it should be. And the *Samadhi* movie spells it out so clearly. My interpretation is that there is no volition to make the present anything other than what it is. The resistance to life is gone. Nothing has changed in the outer world, but nothing is the same 'inside'. No self, no resistance, no attainment. No longer any struggle. Laughingly so. Is this liberation? This is a good word chosen by those before. Yes ... it is liberation from the boundaries created by the ego-mind.

Awareness stays 'inner' until called upon to focus on the 'outer'.

*

More writing later on in the day ...

The parallel universe is *here* and *now*.

I washed that blue doona with the white flowers today and was reminded of the dream, flying into a parallel universe.

So subtle, yet cataclysmic – the shift into a parallel dimension where awareness is free from the mind.

So aptly said previously – there is no choice but to be here and now. It's the way it is.

Mar 26, 2018

Flip flopped

Despite everything written yesterday ...

Today did not seem drastically different from last week, except that the feeling of work abhorrence did not manifest last night or upon waking up (maybe a slight trace).

The feeling that pervaded the day was one of speediness and stomach churning, similar to 'butterflies'. No interpretation was made by the mind, except to note that the feeling was present and a process was occurring.

A challenging situation at work did not perturb the mind's peace in the least; I just floated through it. The whole day was seemingly 'difficult' by past standards, but did not feel so at all.

Don't get me wrong, the mind definitely *tries* to manifest its usual habitual, fearful thoughts. It tries to usurp the moment. What are its habitual thoughts? Strangers showing up, Mum dying, not making enough money. The mind always revisits these themes to elicit an emotional response.

So if this is 'liberation'... it feels very 'normal'. Ha ha. Everything in this parallel universe ...

Ah, so this is what Mum meant when she said it's a flip flop from outer to inner. The parallel universe is the inner, which now is the outer. It's one and the same, but without any boundaries.

Apr 11, 2018

Exhausted

The last day of last week seemed cataclysmic though nothing really happened. This indicates that the interpretation was a mind job ... or the mind was having *another* revolutionary revelation.

Last night, sleep was filled with dreams of death. Death is never scary in the dreams, always peaceful and accepted.

Today there is a feeling that is hard to describe in words. The mind says 'exhaustion'. The word 'broken' pops up or maybe 'bereft', but not in a negative sense, just tired and 'whatever'.

Tonight, I picked the Transformation card from the Osho Zen Tarot deck – ever ongoing.

Words serve to engage the mind, so minimal is best for the moment.

That's all.

May 13, 2018

My teacher

'When the student is ready, the teacher will appear.'

My teacher gave birth to me, literally, spiritually and in every way. Maybe this means I was born 'ready' – whatever that means. My teacher found her teachers, who were also my teachers. Her journey has been my journey.

I came into this life already united with my teacher. So this lifetime must include the journey away from my teacher.

My dream from the other night: I captured a number of sharks and dangerous sea creatures. Then I released them all back into the ocean and watched them swim away free. Only one remained to be released, the mighty Great White, king of sharks. In the dream, I was in the motion of releasing it but did not see it swim away free.

The last Great White yet to be completely released and free. Is this the bond with my teacher (who is also my master and mother)? We are already *one*, but the physical release has not happened. Will this happen prior to one of us dropping the body?

My mother feels the bond. I feel the bond. Neither of us perpetuates it. The bond is there. Spiritually, we are one, but I cannot physically or emotionally leave her. It feels like the only way for the bond to break is when one of us drops the body.

The bond grounds her, and it grounds and binds me. Maybe the bond serves to keep us in our bodies?

The sense is one of being in unforced bondage to my master and not being able to leave. But, when I am alone, the feeling is different – the bondage is not there.

May 14, 2018

Fear

Lately there has been a feeling. This feeling is of separation from that utter freedom, from **the experience** during *that* dream of soaring throughout the universe. That experience is palpable, but somehow not graspable; it is seemingly held away by a thin veil.

The mind is interpreting this pervading feeling as fear. It is a continuation of the feeling that arises every time I am left alone at 'home'. This is the trigger for the feeling.

The feeling envelops my mind like a thick cloud. The mind interprets the cloud as fear … of home invasion, of not feeling safe, of being alone and unable to protect the self, of not being in control, of letting everything go.

It is a fear of losing control. Fear of *letting* go. Fear of that utter freedom of soaring complete and free throughout eternity with no limitations or separations. Ultimately, it is the fear of *death*.

I can feel the veil holding this freedom back – the veil of control. The veil is so thin and ephemeral that the freedom is palpable, but not close enough to experience. So close, but still separate. The mind knows that the veil is illusory. 'I' cannot break out of it. 'I' cannot do anything.

The mind still tries to manipulate right up until what seems like the end, but then more always remains. More remnants, more whiffs of the onion. Who knows if the stinky onion smell will ever disappear? The veil may exist for lifetimes.

Ten minutes later ...

Fear gone

The feeling of fear is gone. As soon as the last entry was written, the fear dissolved.

It's funny how the mind works. As soon as awareness sees beyond the machinations of the mind, the illusion disappears. The tricks of the mind!

The mind cannot understand its own annihilation. The fear of losing its power, fear of becoming nothing, of disappearing, grasping at straws, gasping ...

What happens when the mind is annihilated? This it cannot know or else it will use the knowledge to create another fear or illusion to perpetuate its own survival, like Guerrilla warfare against an illusion.

Oh, the bliss of it. Of disappearing into nothing, where all restraints are gone, where nothing exists, but where everything is perfect. That place in the dream of soaring absolutely free. This is beyond words.

May 16, 2018

More flying

The same night that I wrote my last entry, it seems the writing cleared a barrier for awareness to free flow.

I had another dream two nights ago: I was flying through the cosmos again, this time with a friend holding on to me. At first the flying was slow through the atmosphere. Then I made the decision to fly faster to explore deeper into the emptiness. Acceleration into the unknown. Wow!

Lucid, conscious flying …

May 19, 2018

Samadhi movie, part 2

Part 2 of this movie says everything precisely and succinctly. Nothing more need be said. There is only life to be lived in stillness and silence.

May 23, 2018

Easy

I'm just sitting here on a day off in utter bliss.

The couch is so comfortable. It's a clear, bright blue day outside with more than a hint of breeze. The front loader hums with the laundry cycle. My old dog relaxes on his favourite indoor cushion. A wild rainforest rooster purrs outside the window. *Bliss.* Complete *ease.*

May 24, 2018

Where am I?

Nothing is left.

I went to work today, but had no idea where I was or what I was doing. 'I' was not there. A work colleague asked me several times where I was because she could tell 'I' wasn't there.

Focusing was harder than usual. The day progressed at one speed – slow. A minute felt like an eternity. But I felt more grounded after eating.

Here, but not here. Everywhere.

Spacey. I have to acclimatise to this space.

June 11, 2018

Life

Life always brings what is needed to strip away any vestiges of the illusory self. There need be no questioning this. Losing the garments that define the self – it is a painful process for the mind.

But eventually the mind, as much as it tries, has no more power. No more mind, leaving what?

The space containing life expands, squeezing out every vestige of the unreal. Every moment of expansion brings with it a period of adjustment.* Where is this for the mind? Until consciousness realises that mind is only a tool of perception and not the dictator of who we are … or until mind accepts that it is not in control and never was. And then, as much as one tries to remember what mind (reactivity, emotions) is like, it can't be done. It fades into a memory, a wisp, which itself fades into the awareness that watches it all.

Life serves to bring into our awareness that the mind indeed has no power and shows that there is no self left to react. Poof. All that remains for a moment is the memory (the whiffs) of the habit of reactivity (the onion). Even that becomes an alien concept.

Then what? Then life will show how much power one has *and* how powerless one is. Everything and nothing. The expanse from which life springs, the canvas, the creative ...

*Period of adjustment – every period of expansion of consciousness is followed by a period of adjustment for the mind. Personally, this manifests as an overwhelming, irrational fear of anything the mind can grasp (e.g. death of a loved one, invasion, loss of control).

June 11, 2018

Ramana Maharshi

As Ramana Maharishi says, if something comes and goes, it is not real. If you close your eyes and it disappears, it is not real. That which is real is *always* present. What is always present? (https://www.youtube.com/watch?v=hVYv9ktilQw)

Even during sleep, there is consciousness.

During Ramana's transition, he experienced a great fear of death, which he accepted, and then moved into conscious awareness very quickly!

Ramana stated that we fear the death and loss of loved ones to the same extent as the amount of attachment we have to our own body.

June 12, 2018

Here, but not here

Here but not here.

Not knowing yet always knowing.

None of it – the books, the videos, the words – mean anything to me now. They served their purpose – to help the mind to *let go*.

Yesterday there was no inner reactivity to the events of the day. Outwardly, yes, the mind feebly tried to react the way it was *used* to from its past behaviour. The most unusual dichotomy within ...

An amazing state is manifesting ... consciousness is overshadowing the habitual mental reactivity. When the mind tries to assert some inane thoughts, a deep, powerful 'emptiness' seems to 'push' the thoughts away. This illustrates an experience of which no words could ever describe: the experience of the powerlessness of the mind. Powerlessness *and* substancelessness of the 'mind'.

There is no struggle, just consciousness overriding the habits formed from the mind's memory.

The wisps* of the onion that Mum talks of – *Aha* moment.

*Wisps – the habitual memory of the mind.
*Onion peels – mind.

June 12, 2018

Conscious sleep

For a few weeks, an unusual conscious state has started for me during sleep. During deep, I am conscious . Which 'I' is conscious?

June 14, 2018

New understandings on life and love

Since the turning point on March 19th, I am always aware that life is here and now, and everything else is a fabrication of the mind i.e. thoughts of past and future.

*

What is Nirvana, but the absence of suffering?

*

Are you your mind? Or is your mind you? Find the answer and know your self.

*

We are addicted to thinking, so we believe that we are our thoughts. Once we can let thoughts come and go like clouds in the sky, they will no longer *define* who we are.

*

When the mind is quiet, where is the suffering?

*

What is love, but the complete acceptance of what life brings us?

*

Self-judgement and mental anguish – these are the bane of humanity and the basis of all suffering. There is no other way but to accept and experience life. Then the alchemical transformation takes place within.

*

Do not think that you are alone in your anguish. Every mind suffers, and there are as many minds as there are bodies in the universe.

*

Search for God, search for self, is there a difference? It does not matter where you look, be it in a temple, church, mosque, synagogue or your backyard. Choose where you can find some peace and start there; the rest will come.

*

Be aware of the false teachers. Don't be fooled by someone else's mind telling your mind what to do. Mind is mind and can only bring more anguish.

*

Mortal enemies – our mind versus the natural flow of life. The harder we fight to control and dictate life, the more we suffer.

*

The battle pervades every aspect of existence.

*

When a thought arises, ask the question: Who is thinking? Me, you say. Well, who is 'me'?

*

In your moments of deepest despair, know that it is temporary. A new path is forging in the painful destruction of the old.

6. An Illumined Exploration of Words

Illusion

Caught in a web by a single thread.
Soaring freedom hidden.
Such a large shadow of a minuscule cloud
Blinds the view of YOU,
panorama hazy for a moment.

Until Divine wind blows the wisp away...
Then reality once again ... until the next wisp.

Oh, smelly wisp,
You don't exist!
Only mind makes you real.
You were never a real peel*
How can a stench be so heavy?
Of no-thing, Maya makes a bevy
Of swirling thoughts, oh so petty.

Here we are, never apart,
Yet love makes me forget,
And the suffering begins again.
I am yours always, your plaything, your puppet.
What can I do but suffer the love
Of being yours?

You are here.
Love is here.
Everything is here.
Nothing is here.

Maya, Maya, Maya**,
Why make things so dire?
Tripping us up with your wily ways.

*whiffs of a peeled onion (mind)
**Maya - illusion

Perception and Communication

'Do not feel lonely; the entire universe is inside you.'
– Rumi

'Doors of Perception' – the phrase has so much esoteric and metaphysical meaning, or does it? I first heard the saying in association with Aldous Huxley, a 1950s author who coined the phrase after having wondrous, mind-expanding mescaline mushroom trips. Apparently, after the 'doors of perception' have been opened, we can never go back to seeing things the way they were. Although, this can be an appealing prospect for most of us who are struggling through the grind of daily living.

But the doors of perception are already open in all of us. When our 'I' began to see the world, we stepped through the doors to lose ourselves completely in the illusion of perception. Maybe Huxley was referring to the sense of losing our 'I' momentarily as the drug saturated his synapses.

Stepping through the door of perception is the human tragedy of tragedies – an unavoidable diversion for all sentient beings. The door leads into a maze of the *mind's* world of fantasmagorical *illusion*. The maze does not *exist* anywhere, but within the depths of our minds. The maze of perception is not *real*.

Can we remember when we came into this world, free of any preconceived ideas of how it should be? As a newborn, we could see, touch, hear, feel everything as pure consciousness. We experienced life as it really is, with no expectations or preconceived notions of how it *should* be.

When did we stop experiencing the experience and start labelling the experience? When does the *mind* crystallise itself into a personal being? When does the baby stop being pure *consciousness* and starts being an 'I' with a name? How does it even know to call itself 'I am so and so'?

'I' is a concept born of words to identify the person who is using the words and to describe what they are experiencing. Birth of the 'I' brings with it the birth of *dichotomy*. The self, into I, separate from everything else.

If the experiencer of an experience does not see experiencing as separate from its self, there is no dichotomy. Then the experience is just an experience. Experiences would just be fleeting, ephemeral events if we did not have words. Language allows judgement, interpretation and communication of our experiences. Words facilitate interpretation and solidify judgement.

Interpretation needs a *subject* to interpret the experience and an *object* to experience. Thus the subject, the 'I', is born. The 'I' becomes the experiencer, the communicator, the interpreter – the *perceiver*. The birth of the 'I' coincides with walking through the doors of perception into the maze of an illusory world, of which there are as many I's as there are minds perceiving. *Your interpretation of an experience is yours alone. Your experience of you is your separation from your true self.*

Our initial sensory experience as a newborn is pure and undiluted as we are purely experiencing and not yet interpreting and judging our experiences.. This happens at the *beginning*, before clock time starts to rule our existence, before I, before the *self* comes into being. Every experience after that can only be *compared* with the first experience, thus it loses its purity. *Time* is born then because we always have to refer to the past as a basis of comparison.

Every level of mind machination after the first experience distorts and squashes the experience into our fantasy world of perception. Experience upon experience has a compounding effect:

First experience = *Pure* experience.

Second experience = experience, comparison to the first experience (which becomes the *past*). *Time* is born, and projection starts (*future* is born).

Third experience = experience is no longer pure as the mind has already set up a projection of how it should be based upon the initial experience.

And then we learn words to label these concepts and get: Initial experience, past, future (should, would), etc.

*

Language needs a receptacle to receive our communication, so a *you* is born. We can now communicate our perception to a self outside of our self. So I can tell *you* about *my* experience, and you can tell *me* about *your* experience. The *one* has now split into two: me and the experience, which subsequently splits into four: me and you, my experience and your experience.

You see how the maze gets bigger and more convoluted? As every experience occurs, past history gets bigger, and fodder for future projection grows and grows. The number of experiencers grows infinitely. The initial experience disappears from perception veiled by the illusion of perception and time. Time has distorted experience into a complete fantasy based upon the *past* and projects this onto every subsequent experience making a *future* separate from *now*.

Illusory seconds, minutes, hours, decades, centuries, lifetimes pass. Somewhere along the way, we find a *hint* of the initial experience, which resonates deep within the *consciousness* that has always been there. The veils of perception have covered it layer by layer, but something pierces the veil.

Then we begin our journey back to the *infinite consciousness* from where 'I' was born. Back to the *one*. The *hint* can only be found in the *now*.

Duality

> *'And you? When will you begin your long
> journey into yourself?'*
>
> – Rumi

In the beginning there was *one*, which can also be called, *the true Self*.

How can the one experience itself?

So the one splits into two: the experiencer and the experience.

At this stage, the experiencer is only aware that the experience is occurring, not of a self separate from the experience. Then comes the birth of *duality*.

Duality occurs when the experiencer becomes aware that a presence is experiencing the experience.

What is the experience?

Who is the experiencer?

Identification with an 'I' begins with these questions. *Duality* now has momentum, and *dichotomy* is born.

The 'I' sees itself as separate from the experience. This is the *birth* of the 'I'. The pain of separation begins. The 'I' has become a small *self* unto itself with a need to perpetuate itself. *Fear* is born – the primordial fear of annihilation or death. All other opposites follow.

The pain of separation from the true Self can be repressed, but never eradicated. It becomes the force that eventually compels us to search for who we really are.

The fear of death births all other fears. This is the force that propels the self to exist.

Life = searching for who we really are while simultaneously avoiding our own annihilation.

Silence

'Words, even if they come from the soul, hide the soul.'
– Rumi

silence
ˈsʌɪləns/
noun
noun: silence; plural noun: silences
1. complete absence of sound.

But what is silence? The dictionary can only describe silence as the absence of sound because no words can describe what silence really is. Why?

Because silence lies beyond words. Silence lies beyond the mind using the words.

Silence sounds the way it is. Silent. The absence of sound implies the absence of words, thus the absence of mind. Is this even conceivable? How can the mind grasp what is beyond itself?

The only way to find out about silence is to *be silent*. Quiet the mind, still the movement, cease the activity. Only then does the world beyond the *mind* reveal itself. At first it is a whisper, which grows into a roar if you allow it to reach you.

Silence is the *key* to knowing our true *Self*. Silence only comes when the mind is quiet and our consciousness is completely in the *now*. Then we hear ...

Then we hear that silence is everything. Silence is *full*.

Suffering

'Suffering is a gift – in it is hidden mercy.'
– Rumi

As you read these words, really focus on what is being said here. Can you feel yourself completely present in this moment?

If you are here, you are not thinking of the past, you are not thinking of the future. Are you suffering now?

Can the agony, pain, hopelessness that you are feeling follow you into the *now*? If they do, you are not truly present in the *now*.

So just what is suffering?

The mind is conditioned to live in the past or the future – what I should/could have said or done, what I didn't say or do, what was done to me, what I can't change and regret, what I'm going to do or say. 'Could have', 'Should have', 'Will'....

Living in the past means judgement about events as positive or negative in the context of the self – *self-judgement*, usually negative – self-flagellation, putting the self down. Nothing is ever good enough to the *mind*. This is the nature of the mind. This is the reason for suffering.

The mind will never accept life as it is. Judgement is always there. This is the nature of the mind. The mind wants what it wants. If what the mind wants does not coincide with what *is*, the situation is judged as negative and suffering ensues. If what the mind wants coincides with what is, the mind is happy (for a moment).

The greater the chasm between what is wanted or expected and what actually *is*, the greater the suffering. The mind is always wanting, thus ...

Suffering is the eternal condition of the *mind*.

So we are destined to suffer? Yes.

Until the mind is sick of suffering. And then the search begins; the journey *out of suffering* begins. In other words, suffering is necessary to get rid of the suffering.

Suffering drives us to search for meaning: Who am I? Why am I here? What is it all for?

Why are there so many faiths and people searching for meaning? Because they are suffering.

So, do not despair. You are already on the journey out of your suffering. Breathe in the *now*. See if there is any suffering there.

Mind

'Ever since I was born, I was thrown into this world helpless and shivering like a speck of dust in the air.

But as soon as I reach the end of this journey and settle down, I'll be secured and tranquil forever.'

– Rumi

The *mind*, the pesky mind, the voice that is perpetually moving, talking, bossing, nagging, criticising, judging. The voice inside that never shuts up. The voice that most people believe is *who they are*.

The *mind* is not who *we* are!

Mind perpetually moves. Mind cannot be still. Where there is *stillness* and *silence*, there is *no mind*. But mind is always running away from stillness, running away from silence, fighting its own annihilation. The nature of the mind is perpetual movement – any thought will do, whether positive or negative because ...

Mind needs self-identity, mind needs acknowledgment, mind needs attention. Mind creates drama to escape its own obscurity. Mind creates fantasy to perpetuate itself.

In the beginning, only pure consciousness exists. To perceive life, consciousness develops an 'I', so an 'I' starts to perceive life. The undefined 'I' soon develops an identity separate from the world it experiences, even though the perceiver is not separate from the experience. Experience follows the experiencer, creating the 'I' who we *think* we are, which widens the perceived chasm of our separateness from the original pure consciousness. The experiences we have as a fledgling 'I' help solidify an identity that is fortified by every experience thereafter. Every experience is unique and creates a unique perception of 'I'. No two 'I's are the same.

The experiences that crystallise and solidify the 'I' most powerfully become the keystone of the persona that develops. Jung called these the archetypal events: birth, death, separation from parents, initiation, marriage, etc. These experiences take us away from who we really are – the original pure consciousness – from which none of us are truly separate.

At first, experiences are just experiences. Then we *learn* words and come to understand polarity. Good and bad, pleasant and painful, happy and sad. We learn to judge. Judgement shapes our world – our *fantasy* world. What 'I' feel is 'bad' is only so because I have been conditioned to believe it. Experiences are just experiences until an 'I' labels them as otherwise.

Conditioning solidifies the individual identity. Perception of pain and pleasure are fundamental building blocks for the 'I' or what we call the *ego*.

'I' = self = ego identity = illusion = perception of separateness from the original pure consciousness. *Mind* is the means by which the perceived separation begins and ends.

Bliss

'When you lose all sense of self, the bonds of a thousand chains will vanish.'

– Rumi

The word 'bliss' elicits a response of fevered imagination – perfect happiness, *nirvana*, the ultimate state of ecstasy. If we are thinking of fluffy, pink clouds lined with jewels, beautiful buffets of our favourite foods, an island paradise with azure waters, samadhi, nothing could be further from the actual *truth* of bliss. *Whatever* we imagine bliss to be, nothing would be further from the truth. Why? Because bliss is beyond the *mind*...

What is *bliss*?

Bliss is the absence of suffering. What is suffering? The mind wanting what it wants and finding fault with how things *are*. The absence of suffering means living without the mind's dictation of how things *should* be.

Bliss is complete acceptance of how things are *just as they are* with no judgement. Is that imaginable?

No, not yet, because we imagine with our minds, and the mind cannot imagine an existence without itself. What lies *beyond* the mind? Bliss is the answer.

Bliss, so simple, yet seemingly unattainable. But bliss is always here. This is the paradox. Then why can't we feel it? Because the mind is standing in the way.

We ask: How can we get rid of the mind?

Now the journey into our *self* really begins.

Consciousness, Unconsciousness, Original Mind and Ego

Sleeping and awake. Consciousness and unconsciousness.

So many levels – imagine fractal geometry. So we have the original dual state, which is conscious of the infinite, and the ego-mind state, which is unconscious of the *original self (the true Self)*.

The *origin* is infinite unconsciousness and infinite consciousness experienced through *pure mind* that is devoid of ego-mind and identity as a separate self. This is manifested in a gross form, which initially sees itself as a separate *entity* that can control its existence by using the ego-mind.

To elaborate further, I will give you a summary of Meher Baba's* elucidation:

Ego-mind develops via samskaras or impressions that define the separate identity of the manifestation. These impressions start accruing from the first form of manifestation – gas, mineral, stone, insect, fish, reptile, bird, mammal and, finally, human. These impressions define the qualities of a human incarnation and the reality in which they live. Each life impressions accrue and unwind similar to opposite sides of a mathematical sum – one side holding the positive impressions, and the other side holding the negative impressions. As long as the amount on each side of the equation is unequal, the 'soul' has to *reincarnate* to play out the impressions. Only when the negative impressions and positive impressions cancel each other out, can the 'soul' be freed from the endless cycle of separateness from the *original* state.

This journey of involution involves three planes: *gross, subtle* and *mental*. The entity identifies with the gross body and lives as such until it plays out its need to experience everything in the gross form. Then it moves to the subtle body and plays out experiences in this form. Then it lives life through the mental body. At a point, the entity has played out enough that it realises it is not its gross body, its subtle body or its mental body and searches for its true self. True suffering, for the entity, is knowing that existence is not this or not that, but not knowing what it really is.

The movement from gross to subtle to mental existences is the searching for *Self* as the impressions come closer and closer to wearing themselves out.

*

More play on words for today ...

The veil separating the small ego-self of a being from the true *original self* is made from a fabric of accrued impressions. As these impressions wear out, the veil becomes thinner and thinner. Glimpses of the *true self* are experienced and serve to increase the feeling of separateness of the self. This manifests as the ultimate suffering and desire for *union* with the *self.*

When the impressions are worn out, the being realises that it is not separate from the *original self.* The suffering ceases, but the being has no experience of *self* and instead experiences the *divine vacuum* where *nothing* exists, nothing has meaning. It sees nothing, experiences nothing, knows nothing and is nothing. The being no longer exists. The being is *no self.* Memories linger of impressions and existence continues where the entity acts like the old separate self in accordance with habitual behaviour (memories of self) but it is surrounded by *nothingness.*

The divine vacuum remains until a fraction of a moment when the *no self* experiences the *original self* in the dual state of infinite consciousness and infinite unconsciousness. The understanding slowly crystallises and the *no self* begins experiencing itself as the *original self*. This experience deepens and deepens infinitely as the *origin* has no beginning or end.

* Meher Baba – a Self-realised Indian Master

Awareness

My experience has changed since my entry about *perception*. There is no longer perception because: The dichotomy between the *beyond, Beyond* the *beyond* and *here* is no longer the experience.

There is no origin as such. The origin is not separate from here. *All is here*, so it can't be two separate words. So let us choose a word that includes both.

The origin is always present, beyond time. There's no linearity. The moment as perceived by the mind-state is always original.

Awareness.

Perceiving is from *consciousness*, which is of the *mind*.

Within *awareness* (A) everything is present, yet nothingness is also ubiquitous.

'A' can be described as a singularity – one and also infinite, simultaneously. (Definition of singularity: the condition of being singular or a point at which a function takes an infinite value, especially in space–time when matter is infinitely dense, such as at the centre of a black hole).

'A' watches the illusory mind ebb and flow, scrambling for understanding and playing out all the threads of samskaras. 'A' is not the *mind* and it cannot be defined by the *mind*. Actually, mind is just a tool of perception. It is the only means by which 'A' can filter experiences using the senses.

This mind-state, place, experience is empty, full, still, moving. On a human level, anxiety does not exist as an ongoing experience (incidental bodily stress, a momentary fight or flight is still present), attachments seem to have disintegrated.

Description of *awareness* – a type of ambivalence, neutrality, an emotionless state when the mind-state is not elicited, but becomes entirely humanly focused which is when the mind-state activates. It can be described as awareness until engagement.

The mind-state then asks what is the purpose of its existence because it thinks that it is real. At this stage while writing this, it realises that only the *awareness* is real and the mind-state is only a state of concentration of 'A'. The mind-state is the state of 'A' focusing through perception of the senses.

There is no place other than now; all other places, states and times are illusions created when the *mind* forgets that it is just a tool, starts to try to define the self and makes a separate entity of itself.

Awareness is our natural state until focus is needed. Then mind-state is elicited to focus, crystallise and perceive interaction with gross life.

KNOWLEDGE POWER BLISS

7. Epilogue

Jul 24, 2018

That is all for the moment. The journey continues. The silent spaces are getting longer and longer. The pesky mind is a brat and will always try to find something to sink its teeth into and be worried about. So I'm ever vigilant on that front.

The angst and anxiety that plagued me for years has not arisen since the day that everything imploded but nothing really happened (Mar 19, 2018).

The feeling of separateness is gone. The moments are empty, yet full.

Life is the same as before – working, eating, sleeping, exercising, hanging out – but it is fundamentally different. I can't say that it is blissful or peaceful, but there is no angst, no worry, no anxiety and *that* in itself makes it *nirvana*!

What is different? My guess is that the mind was so bereft and tortured from trying to keep control of everything that it surrendered in exhaustion. It just gave up in complete resignation.

Every now and then, it pokes its nose up and tries to interfere, but when it does, something infinitely wiser takes charge now.

The story has no beginning or end. Maybe there will be a second book of adventures, we will see.

E.M. Martin

Poem 10

So it goes on ...

Tibetans bell rings three.
Nothing left of me.
Mind can finally see
the utter futility

Movement ceases.
Wisps disappear.
Mind stills.
Space fills
... with Divinity

For the moment ...

ABOUT THE AUTHOR

Educated in Singapore, Hawaii, Paris and Australia, Dr E.M. Martin is the consummate professional and holds three university degrees, including one in the medical science field. Raised in a spiritually aware family, she has been meditating since the age of fifteen. Meditation gave her glimpses into a deeper reality, so she has travelled to the far reaches of her outer and inner worlds, searching for the answers to life's greater questions.

Enjoyed the book?

You can leave a review on Goodreads at
https://www.goodreads.com/amazon

You can follow the author at
www.emmartin.live

and connect with her on
https://www.facebook.com/JourneyBeyondTheSelf

Journey Beyond the Self 113

www.ingramcontent.com/pod-product-compliance
Lightning Source LLC
Chambersburg PA
CBHW061111010526
44110CB00062B/2669